BUREAU FOR PARANORMAL · RESEARCH AND DEFENSE ·

THE SOUL OF VENICE
& OTHER STORIES

Created by MIKE MIGNOLA

JOHANN KRAUS

A medium whose physical form was destroyed while his ectoplasmic projection was out-of-body. That essence now resides in a containment suit. A psychic empath, Johann can create temporary forms for the dead to speak to the living.

LIZ SHERMAN

A fire-starter since the age of 11, when she accidentally burned her entire family to death. She has been a ward of the B.P.R.D. since then, learning to control her pyrokinetic abilities and cope with the trauma those abilities have wrought.

ABE SAPIEN

An amphibious man discovered in a long-forgotten subbasement beneath a Washington, D.C. hospital sealed inside a primitive stasis chamber. All indications suggest a previous life, dating back to the Civil War—an unfolding mystery for Abe.

ROGER

A homunculus made from human blood and herbs. Discovered in Romania, Roger was first brought to life by Liz's pyrokinetic touch. Whether or not he is actually alive may be up for debate, but his child-like love of that life is not.

DR. KATE CORRIGAN

A former professor at New York University, an authority on folklore and occult history. Dr. Corrigan has been a B.P.R.D. consultant for over 10 years, now serving as special liaison to the enhanced-talents task force.

Mike Mignola's

B.P.R.D.™

THE SOUL OF VENICE
& OTHER STORIES

Featuring

MIKE MIGNOLA, MILES GUNTHER

MICHAEL AVON OEMING, BRIAN AUGUSTYN

GUY DAVIS, GEOFF JOHNS

SCOTT KOLINS, JOE HARRIS

ADAM POLLINA, & CAMERON STEWART

Editor
SCOTT ALLIE

Assistant Editor
MATT DRYER

Collection Designer
RICHARD E. JONES

Publisher
MIKE RICHARDSON

DARK HORSE BOOKS™

NEIL HANKERSON ♦ *executive vice president*

TOM WEDDLE ♦ *vice president of finance*

RANDY STRADLEY ♦ *vice president of publishing*

CHRIS WARNER ♦ *senior books editor*

ANITA NELSON ♦ *vice president of sales & marketing*

MICHAEL MARTENS ♦ *vice president of business development*

DAVID SCROGGY ♦ *vice president of product development*

LIA RIBACCHI ♦ *art director*

DALE LaFOUNTAIN ♦ *vice president of information technology*

DARLENE VOGEL ♦ *director of purchasing*

KEN LIZZI ♦ *general counsel*

Published by Dark Horse Books
A division of Dark Horse Comics, Inc.
10956 SE Main Street
Milwaukie, OR 97222

First edition August 2004
ISBN: 1-59307-132-9

1 3 5 7 9 10 8 6 4 2

Printed in China

This book collects the B.P.R.D. oneshots *The Soul of Venice, Dark Waters, Night Train,*
and *There's Something Under My Bed*, published by Dark Horse Comics.

THE SOUL OF VENICE

THE SOUL OF VENICE

Story by
MILES GUNTHER & MICHAEL AVON OEMING
with MIKE MIGNOLA

Art by
MICHAEL AVON OEMING

Colors by
DAVE STEWART

Letters by
KEN BRUZENAK

O Cloacina,
    goddess of this place
Look on thy servant
    with a smiling face
Oft and cohesive
    let my offering flow
Not rudely swift
    nor obstinately slow

ABE, WHY THE LONG FACE?

I'VE BEEN HERE BEFORE.

THAT GOOD HUH?

"IT WASN'T EXACTLY THE PLATONIC IDEAL I'D ENVISIONED.

"THE WATER WAS SO POLLUTED THAT WHEN I DOVE IN... I...

"I COULDN'T COME OUT OF MY TANK FOR A MONTH AFTER THAT."

THIS IS WHY YOU BROUGHT YOUR TUB.

YEAH, IF I HAVE TO GET BACK IN THERE, I'M GOING TO NEED A BATH.

JOHANN, DO YOU SENSE ANYTHING? MAYBE WE CAN PINPOINT THE CENTER OF THIS MESS.

YES... I WILL TRY.

BLAM!
BLAM!
BLAM!

click!
click!

DAMN!

FOOLISH CREATURES!

THERE IS NO ESCAPE.

CLOACINA,

DARK WATERS

DARK WATERS

Story by
BRIAN AUGUSTYN

Art by
GUY DAVIS

Colors by
DAVE STEWART

Letters by
MICHELLE MADSEN

IN ADDITION TO THE *BODIES*, WE FOUND SEVERAL INTERESTING . . . *ARTIFACTS*.

THE REMAINS OF WHAT TURNED OUT TO BE ANCIENT *DEVICES*-- A STOCKS, LEG IRONS, A *DUNKING STOOL* . . .

TORTURE DEVICES ASSOCIATED WITH *WITCH TRIALS*.

SO . . . YOU'RE THE *CHIEF*.

JOB'S BEEN IN THE FAMILY FOR GENERATIONS. I GOT ELECTED 'CAUSE FOLKS GOT *USED* TO VOTING FOR A RACKHAM.

ANNE RACKHAM CHIEF CONSTABLE

AS YOU CAN SEE, IT IS AN *ELEGANT* AND *PRESTIGIOUS* JOB.

REVEREND LUCAS SHAW, THIS IS ABE SAPIEN AND . . . UM . . . ROGER . . . FROM THE B.P.R.D.

LUKE'S THE MINISTER OVER TO OLD STONE CHURCH. IT'S OLDER EVEN THAN THE TOWN . . .

. . . AND IT'S *HISTORICAL* RECORDS ARE *BETTER*. I ASKED HIM TO LOOK INTO THIS *WITCH* QUESTION.

THERE'S NOT MUCH . . . AND THEN YOU HAVE TO READ BETWEEN THE LINES . . .

. . . BUT SHILOH *DID* HAVE A *WITCH PROBLEM*.

OR RATHER, THEY GOT CAUGHT UP IN THE *SALEM* HYSTERIA, AND *THOUGHT* THEY DID. THIS WAS BACK IN *1693*.

THREE SISTERS, PRISCILLA, PRUDENCE, AND POLLYANNE TRASK, WERE ACCUSED OF *BLACK MAGIC*. SEEMS THEY GREW PRIZE ROSES WHILE EVERYONE ELSE GOT *THORNS*.

THEY WERE ARRESTED, TRIED, AND *TESTED* FOR *WITCHCRAFT*.

'COURSE NOW, UNDERSTAND, THIS TEST WASN'T ONE *ANYONE* COULD PASS, REALLY.

"BOUND AND WEIGHTED WITH CHAINS, THE ACCUSED WERE THROWN INTO A BODY OF WATER . . .

" . . . IF THEY *SUNK* THEY WERE INNOCENT.

"OF COURSE THEY WERE ALSO *DEAD*.

"THUS BEGAN-- AND *ENDED*--SHILOH'S BRIEF FLING WITH WITCH HYSTERIA."

SHAMED BY WHAT THEY'D DONE, APPARENTLY, THE TOWNSFOLK DUMPED EVERYTHING CONNECTED WITH THEIR CRIMES IN THE POND TOO . . . AND *BURIED* THEIR SIN.

AND *NOW* WE'VE FOUND IT. THANKS, LUKE. COME ON, GENTS, LET'S GET YOU A LOOK AT OUR *POND*.

NIGHT TRAIN

NIGHT TRAIN

Story by
GEOFF JOHNS & SCOTT KOLINS

Art by
SCOTT KOLINS & DAVE STEWART

Letters by
PAT BROSSEAU

RRRRRRR--

WHEEET

GO. RUN. *NOW.*

JUSTICE HAS WAITED LONG ENOUGH...

NO! PLEASE LISTEN. YOU'VE GOT THE *WRONG GUY!*

SHE IS *NOT* HIM!

THERE'S SOMETHING UNDER MY BED

THERE'S SOMETHING UNDER MY BED

Story by
JOE HARRIS

Pencils by
ADAM POLLINA

Inks by
GUILLERMO ZUBIAGA

Colors by
LEE LOUGHRIDGE

Letters by
PAT BROSSEAU

BOBBBBBBEEEEEEEEEEEE...

YOU'VE HEARD ABOUT BOBBY MCKENNA AND THE OTHER CHILDREN. I KNOW THIS IS ALL A LITTLE DIFFICULT TO ACCEPT, BUT YOU HAVE TO *TRUST* US.

WE HAVE NO WAY OF *PREDICTING* WHERE THE NEXT ABDUCTION ATTEMPT MIGHT OCCUR. OR TO WHOM, SPECIFICALLY.

BUT WE HAVE *EVERY* INTENTION OF KEEPING YOUR DAUGHTER SAFE.

IS THAT ALL RIGHT, LIEBSCIEN?

YOU... HAVE TO *EXCUSE* EMILY...

WE...I MEAN... *SHE* ISN'T USED TO COMPANY--

--LIKE *YOU* PEOPLE--

--WE MEAN.

I UNDER-STAND ENTIRELY.

I LOOK AT MYSELF IN THE *MIRROR*, SOME MORNINGS, AND I SEE WHAT *YOU* DO. THERE IS NO OFFENSE.

BUT IN *MY* LINE OF WORK, I FIND IT IMPORTANT TO RE-MEMBER THAT IT IS *ONE* THING TO BE A *MONSTER*--

WUBBAFLIES!

--WHILE BEING *MONSTROUS* IS SOMETHING ELSE, ENTIRELY.

GO.

IT--IT'S GETTING LATE, PRINCESS. LET'S SAY GOOD-NIGHT TO OUR, UM--

SAY GOODNIGHT TO OUR GUESTS, SWEETIE, AND LET'S GET YOU READY FOR BED.

BUT I'M NOT *SLEEPY*, DADDY. ≥YAWN≥

THEN WHO'S THAT CLOSING THOSE BEAUTIFUL BLUE EYES?

THAT'S A GOOD GIRL.

ANOTHER DAY AT THE OFFICE

Story by
MIKE MIGNOLA

Art by
CAMERON STEWART

Colors by
MICHELLE MADSEN

Letters by
MICHAEL HEISLER

RARARARR

GRRRRRR

HMM.

TOLD YA.

APPARENTLY A BUNCH OF THEM WANDERED INTO TOWN YESTERDAY...

"...BUT THE LOCALS TOOK CARE OF THEM..."

BY THE TIME WE GOT HERE THERE WAS JUST THIS ONE LEFT. HE WAS HIDING IN A BUSH.

JOHANN?

THIS MAN DIED A NATURAL DEATH. HIS SPIRIT HAS PASSED OVER.

BUT THERE IS SOMETHING...

48 MINUTES LATER.

COUNT YEGOR KURYA. BLOODTHIRSTY TYRANT. NATIONAL HERO. THE USUAL STUFF. HE BUILT THIS MONASTERY IN 1448...

...AND HE WAS BURIED HERE AFTE HIS ASSASSINATION.

THERE'S ALSO A LEGEND ABOUT THIS PLACE AND A HIDDEN TREASURE.

OF COURSE.

HEY LOOK...

ZOMBIES.

THUD

WELL, THAT WASN'T TOO BAD.

WE'RE GONNA NEED A TRUCK.

IT SEEMS ROBERT HUNTLEY HAS A PSYCHIC GIFT...BUT HE WAS UNAWARE OF IT UNTIL HE DISTURBED KURYA'S REMAINS. THEN KURYA, THE DOMINANT PERSONALITY, MADE USE OF THAT GIFT TO REANIMATE THE RECENTLY DEAD.

BLOODTHIRSTY TYRANT TO BONES ON A ROPE...

"...IT WAS A BAD DAY FOR YEGOR KURYA."

THE END

B.P.R.D.

SKETCHBOOK

These pages feature sketchbook material from all the artists included in *The Soul of Venice and Other Stories*. While the book is *B.P.R.D.*, artists do tend to fill their sketchbooks with images of Hellboy.

—Scott Allie

To me, Hellboy is the one of the best creations in at least the last forty years. Getting to work on anything Hellboy-related, like *Night Train*, will always be a dream come true. I was smiling as I drew every line of this book. A big thank you to Mike Mignola, Scott Allie, Matt Dryer, Jeremy Barlow, Pat Brosseau, Dave Stewart, my bud Geoff Johns, and everyone at Dark Horse. These are some of my page breakdowns and sketches.

—Scott Kolins

When I first saw Mignola's Hellboy—the one where he fights the giant dog at the gas station—I thought the same thing everyone else did: "Wow, that's cool, he wears goggles." It was a neat time, discovering Hellboy. I'd been a fan of Mike's since *Cosmic Odyssey* and watched him progress over the years. Now he was doing something uniquely him. Amazing stuff. Soon, this layered creation started to uncover itself, layers of mystery. First the visuals—Mike's use of black, the mood within his art. The environment, the backgrounds, that strange, semi-Victorian feel to his work. All that was new to me then, and the work shares a special place in my life with other great stories that reveal themselves in their freshness, and then sustain themselves over the years.

I was lucky enough to get to know Mike some, so when the chance came to work on *Soul of Venice*, not only did I want to impress the artist, but I wanted to make sure Mike the man was happy, too. He worked with us on the layout, and especially the cover, adding his own touch. Sitting in his studio, surrounded by books and unpublished Mignola art as he doodled on my layouts, is one of the best memories I've had in comics.

Mike—On behalf of myself, Kelsey, and Miles, I thank you for such a great character and world, and allowing us to play with them.

—Michael Avon Oeming

Even though his story doesn't feature Lobster
Johnson, Oeming loves the character so much
he couldn't restrain himself.

—Scott Allie

Art by
Adam Pollina

Unlike some of the other franchises we've had the privilege of working on in comics, something about Hellboy and the B.P.R.D. feels just as classic as the X-Men, etc., while feeling incredibly fresh and new at the same time. Both Adam and I were thrilled to bring our twisted mix of horror and playtime to the table.

—Joe Harris

Mike's imagination and design has always been an inspiration, so I jumped at the chance to try my hand at drawing his characters—who wouldn't? Even a mundane backdrop like the small Massachusetts town in *Dark Waters* was entertaining to draw with the likes of Abe and Roger poking around in it. Aside from giving Abe a sleeveless rain coat, most of the new designs needed were centered on the mud men and giant muckworm. Both were pretty straightforward; the muckworm itself was toned down a bit in the finished art.

—Guy Davis

I've been a fan of *Hellboy* for the last ten years, and a fan of Mike Mignola for even longer, so being asked to contribute to this universe was both a thrill and an honor. I was kindly asked what sort of story I wanted to draw and decided that something to do with European zombies would be the most fun. Presented here are some of the preliminary sketches and rough layouts I produced for the story—if you compare the layouts with the final pages you can see a lot of changes based on Mike and Scott's suggestions.

—Cameron Stewart

HELLBOY

by MIKE MIGNOLA